ICELAND

GREENLAND

N

W E

S

Northwest
Passage

Baffin

Bay

Ellesmere Island

Baffin Island

Labrador
Sea

Atlantic

Ocean

TERRITORIES

Cape
Dorset

A D A

NEWFOUNDLAND

Hudson

Bay

tree line

QUEBEC

Gulf
of
St. Lawrence

PRINCE EDWARD
ISLAND
fishing

St. Lawrence

Laurentian Mountains

NOVA
SCOTIA

ONTARIO

maple
sugar

St. Lawrence

Quebec

Montreal

NEW
BRUNSWICK

Ottawa

Lake
Champlain

Toronto

Windsor

AMERICA

CANADA: GIANT NATION OF THE NORTH

takes us on a journey through a young giant of a country — one of the world's great storehouses of natural resources. The challenge and promise of scarcely tapped natural wealth make Canada one of the few real frontier regions left on earth.

We visit small fishing villages, mining towns, lumber camps, prairie wheat farms, large industrial cities, and vast arctic and sub-arctic regions. Stories, legends, and interesting informative chapters take us into family circles of varying racial backgrounds. We meet the Indians who trap mink and beaver in the winter and return for trading and schooling in the summer. We also look in on Eskimo families, an important people to Canada, for they know the arctic regions as few white men do.

The individual flavor of the book is enhanced by paintings and drawings by some of Canada's leading illustrators through the cooperation of the Canadian Society of Book Illustrators.

Pictures by Canadian Artists:

Aileen T. Richardson and William J. Wheeler

CANADA

GIANT NATION OF THE NORTH

By JANE WERNER WATSON

GARRARD PUBLISHING COMPANY   CHAMPAIGN, ILLINOIS

Acknowledgments

The paintings and drawings in this book have been done especially for it by Canadian illustrators Aileen T. Richardson and William J. Wheeler. Mr. Wheeler illustrated "North Is the Future" and "Northwest Passage." Miss Richardson illustrated "Petit Jacques" and "Gypsy Show" and did the other scattered illustrations.

The endsheet map of Canada is by James A. Bier. The cover painting of a Great Lakes grain port and back cover spot of a Pacific Coast totem pole are by William J. Wheeler.

Photo credits:

Eleanor Burt for Lake Louise, Alberta, page 32

Canadian Government Travel Bureau for photos by:
Malak of White Pass and Yukon Route Railroad, title page; J. de Visser of oil refinery in Moosjaw, Saskatchewan, page 28; E. Bork of wheat fields and grain elevators, Killaly, Saskatchewan, page 48; M. Milne of Montreal and harbor from the air, page 53; R. Halin of children playing in Jasper, Alberta schoolyard, page 88; J. de Visser of railroad center, Winnipeg, Manitoba, page 92

National Film Board of Canada for photos by:
D. Wilkinson of Eskimo hunters of Northwest Territories, page 24; J. Sproat of Eskimo children of Northwest Territories at school in Cape Dorset, page 26; E. Bork of loggers in booming area, Lake Superior, Ontario, page 33; Ted Grant of logging trucks being loaded, British Columbia, page 35; Chris Lund of Parliament Building, Ottawa, Ontario, page 83; Chris Lund of construction of a chemical plant in New Brunswick, page 97; G. Hunter of helicopters on geological survey in Yukon, page 99

New Brunswick Travel Bureau for:
haying scene, page 56; fishing boats and lobster pots, page 57; fishermen with herring catch, page 68

Robert P. Sharp for Ice Field Ranges, page 30

Susan S. Sweezy for Ontario pulp mill, page 37

Cover art by William J. Wheeler

Contents

A Story

1. North Is the Future

Bad News

My name is Derek Mackenzie. I will tell you about the worst time of my life.

First I have to explain that I live in a mining town in the Northwest Territories, where my father is a mining engineer. We used to live down in Calgary, which is a rather large city. My mother was not very keen to come up here.

My dad said to her, "Fran, the future is in the North. I will not get far in the company unless I know the arctic part of the operation. This move is for only two years. The company will provide a house and a food allowance, and

there is radio-telephone service. We get a free
flight south at the end of a year for our holiday.
We can save toward that house you want in
Westgate." (Westgate is a pretty part of Calgary,
where lots of Mother and Dad's friends live.)
"It will be a great experience for the children
and for us all," my dad said.

So Mother packed up, and we flew to the Arctic.
We had flown before, to Montreal to visit my
uncle, but this was different. The plane was
smaller, for one thing. There was not much to
see down below—no towns or fields or highways.
For miles and miles there were dark trees. Then
there was just pale ground spotted with water
that glittered when the sun struck it right.

"A lot of nothing much," Mother said. And
I saw her shiver. Maybe she already had a
feeling of that worst time that was coming.

When we circled down over the town, we could
see the mine buildings, the slag heaps, the rows
of houses, and the harbor on the bay. The houses
looked like Mark's building blocks, yellow and
pink and blue. Oh, I should tell you that Mark
is my small brother and I have a sister Leila, too.

All the houses were square and the same size.

We were surprised to see that they were raised off the ground.

"That's because of the permafrost," Dad explained. "Up here the frost goes down into the ground for hundreds of feet. If a house is built on the ground and the building is heated, the ground warms up too. The surface of the permafrost melts into deep mud. The building settles down in the soft muck and its walls and floors crack."

We saw that all the buildings had long thin boxes running from one to another. Those boxes held all the pipes for water, sewage, and heat— also the wires for electricity.

When we landed, we were surprised at how hot the Arctic was in late June.

I said, "It's late afternoon, so let's hurry with our luggage so we can go down to the harbor and see the boats before it gets dark."

Dad laughed. "You're almost in the 'Land of the Midnight Sun,' my lad," he said. "The sun won't go down until eleven o'clock tonight, and it will be up again by one in the morning."

It seemed strange to go to sleep with the curtains drawn, while the sun shone brightly outside.

But that soon changed, for every day the sun went down a few minutes earlier.

By November, it was just poking up over the horizon in the late morning.

We could look out the windows of our schoolroom and see the sun rise. Over on Leila's side of the school, they could watch it set early in the afternoon. It was deep blue twilight when we went to school in the morning, and again when we returned home, crunching over the thin snow.

Another thing surprised us; there was not nearly as much snow as we used to have in Calgary, but still it was too cold to play outside.

We missed a lot of things about Calgary. We missed jumping into the car to go somewhere, since there were no roads around our new town. We missed television, and ice hockey games in the big stadium. And during the summer, oh, how we had missed the excitement of Stampede Week, with cowboys and rodeos, fireworks and Indian dances, and a real Indian camp. Stampede Week is a great time.

One thing that was nice, though, was having Dad home so much to play with us. In the evenings we would turn on the radio or play

records, and Dad and Mother often played games with us.

Sometimes Dad had to go off on trips. Mother didn't say much, but we knew she didn't like it when he flew away in one of the little company planes. She always started sewing or knitting when Dad went away. You never saw her without something in her hands.

It was one of these trips that caused our worst time.

I didn't know about it as soon as some. In the middle of the morning, we were busy at school with seatwork. I heard the door open, and Kiakshuk, the Eskimo teaching assistant, came in.

He is great, Kiakshuk is, very good at softball and netball. He is smiling, quiet and easy, but nobody argues when Kiakshuk is in charge of the game. He is a little bit like Dad that way.

Well, that morning Kiakshuk went very quietly up to the teacher's desk. He spoke to Mr. Dinwiddie, our teacher. Mr. Dinwiddie looked up, startled. He looked at me, then looked away.

I wondered for a minute, but soon history period started and we were busy, so I didn't know anything until we got home for lunch.

Mother came to the door. She smiled at us, but her eyes looked pink around the edges. Mrs. Kucek from next door was there. Her eyes looked pink too, but she started dishing up the soup.

I was about to ask, "When does Dad get in?" I knew he was due home. But something stopped me. "What's wrong?" I asked instead.

Mother was making hard work of unfolding her napkin.

"Dad will be—delayed," she said. "The plane didn't reach the last settlement. It probably had engine trouble."

That was the beginning of the worst time in my life. Dad and Dave Benson, the company pilot, had crashed in the icy wasteland. They might never come home.

Survival

My name is Roger Mackenzie. I'm a mining engineer in the Northwest Territories, and part of my work is checking out claims, so I'm used to flying. We all have training in what to do in case of a crash landing. Survival training, it is called. These bush pilots are really skillful though. They take care of their planes as if they were babies, so we don't think much about accidents.

As we flew over the tundra that morning, I was not thinking of anything but the report in my briefcase, and getting home to my wife Fran and the children, Derek, Mark, and Leila.

Then I felt the plane jerk. I looked out the side window of the cockpit. A puff of flame shot out of the port engine. Then came another puff.

Dave Benson, the pilot, muttered something under his breath and snapped off a switch. The flame flared up, then died. The propeller stopped.

"Have to go down," said Dave in his slow drawl.

He had the plane steady again. We slipped in for a nice landing on a snow field that looked level enough. But a bump under the snow caught the right ski. The plane spun around and one wing crumpled and tore.

In the landing one of Dave's legs was caught and a bone cracked below the knee, so it was up to me to fix a shelter. I bandaged his leg with a splint as well as I could, then set to work.

I should tell you that this was late March, so fortunately we did have some daylight to work in. A month before, in February, there would have been just a few minutes of rosy dawn, then sunset, twilight, and night again.

I fastened my parka and climbed out onto the good wing to survey our surroundings. Not far away I could see the dark ice of the bay. That was good, I figured. Perhaps we could have fish.

Off the other way I saw a clump of low brush, brown and dry against the snow. That was good; we would need all the firewood we could get.

We were north of the tree line, so I couldn't build a shelter of branches. The snow was not thick enough for me to build a snow house. But the plane would give us material for a shelter from the wind and should help to keep up a good fire.

I hunched into the wind and fought my way over to the clump of brush. I cut as much as I could drag.

Back at the plane, I piled the firewood on the lee side, where the fuselage would shelter us from the wind. The crumpled wing made part of a

wall. A couple of empty crates from the plane helped too. We had some bundles of fur pelts from one of the trappers' settlements, and I dragged those down for beds.

When the shelter was finished, three-sided and roofed with the good wing, I helped Dave down. He had to be near the fire.

By that time it was dark, but we had enough brushwood to keep a small blaze going for the long night. Dave always carries a can of water in the plane, and of course we could boil snow. We both had kits of food, so I opened a can of beans and boiled water for coffee. After we had finished a meal of canned beans, we took turns getting what sleep we could. One of us had to be awake to keep the fire going.

When the dark lightened to twilight, which meant that day had come, I set off again for another clump of brush. I did not want to burn anything from the plane if I could help it, but we had to keep that fire going.

Then, leaving some brushwood within reach of Dave's arm, I started for the bay to try fishing. Dave had said he would fix up a snare for me to set for arctic hare, if I could find some tracks.

14

I am not much of a hunter, but I have fished all my life. So down to the bay I went.

On the way to the bay, I crossed a big, level snowfield. My tracks stretching out behind me made me think of a signal, so I tramped out a giant H E L P in the dry snow.

Down at the bay I found a crack in the thick ice big enough for a fish, and dropped my line down. I had some fish hooks from Dave's emergency kit, and a couple of flies. I'd never heard of ice-fishing with dry flies, but I tried. Soon a nice arctic char obliged me by nibbling.

We had fish baked in the ashes for dinner, and it tasted good. I set the snare Dave had made, where I found some small tracks in the snow. And I scouted for more brush for the fire. Clumps of brush were scarce in those parts, though, and I dared not go too far from the plane.

Soon it was too dark to hunt, so we settled our camp for another night. The day had been easier for me than for Dave because I had kept busy, but still I kept thinking of Fran and the children.

Dave had tried the radio after landing, but with no luck.

"Tomorrow I've got to get back into the cockpit and get to work on that radio," he said.

I nodded. This was not the kind of country where roots and berries could keep us going.

We melted some more snow for coffee, pulled the trappers' pelts around us, eased a little more brush onto the fire, and settled down for another night.

We did not say so, but I know we both hoped there would not be many more nights out there for us. We thought of men we knew who had been lost in the Arctic, and we both wondered if we would ever get back home.

Rescue

My name is Kiakshuk. I belong to "The People," *Innuit* in our language. Men from the south call us Eskimos.

I went away to a school, and now I am an assistant teacher. Four days each week I teach in the school in town. Then on Friday mornings I have tea early, and my friend and I load boxes of supplies onto a dog sled. We put our sleeping bags and rifles on top. My friend cracks his 45-foot-long whip. As it snaps like a flame in

16

the air, we jump on top of the load, and off the huskies go!

Twenty-five miles north from the town is the camp where I teach my people. All day I teach the children; in the evening the parents and old people come to learn to read and write.

When the lessons are over, we sit and talk. They tell me the news of the camp. My older brother is talking of buying a snow buggy with a motor for visiting his traps, to take the place of his dogsled and huskies. My younger brother wants a new outboard motor for his fishing boat, when the ice breaks up this year. The brother of my father shows me some animals he has carved from walrus tusks and soapstone. I will carry them to the trading post for the man there to sell.

I tell them the news of the town. One of the mining company's planes is missing. It went down somewhere on the snow. The father of one of the boys I teach, a boy named Derek, was on this plane. I think of the boy's sad face. I tell how my friend and I looked on every side for the plane on our way to the camp. . . .

As we circled the bay heading north from the town, the shore rose in cliffs. There we walked to help the dogs pull the loaded sled up the slope. We had time to look on all sides, but there was no plane to be seen.

Beyond the cliffs, the land dropped again. We hopped onto the sled and dragged our feet to keep it from going too fast. We still peered on all sides through our slit snow goggles for a sign of the missing plane.

Here the land curved softly away to the sky on all sides, and we could see a long way. We watched the moon sink into the icy bay. The deep blue sky turned pale. Then the sun rose in a red ball, but still we could see no dark shape on the snow.

My people listened as I told the tale. The

mother of my brother's wife was among them. She is a very old woman with wrinkled skin, but her eyes are bright and she is very wise. Every spring she tells us what day the ice will break up, and it always breaks up on that day. In the summer, when boats come on the bay, she tells us how far away each supply boat is, and it appears just when she says it will.

Now as I spoke of the lost plane, she sucked on her pipe and closed her bright eyes.

"I have seen this plane," she said. She spoke in the language of my people. "I have seen it down on the snow. It is near the bay, not very far from here." She waved her pipe to the north.

That is all she would say. She sucked on her pipe again.

I did not sleep well that night. I thought of

the pilot and the father of Derek, out in the wind and cold.

As soon as the camp stirred, I was ready to leave. I drank a cup of something hot. Then I stepped into my fur boots and parka. My friend brought the dogsled and cracked his long whip. We hopped onto the sled and were off.

We did not head back to town but went along the bay shore to the north. We climbed to the highest point of the hilly shore, walking behind the sled, but there was nothing to be seen.

We hopped back onto the sled, and the dogs raced away down the hill. The sky turned pink, the sun rose, another day lightened.

We knew we could not go much farther; we must turn back toward the town. But one last hill we would climb, before turning back.

Up we went. Again I peered all around through my slit snow goggles, but I saw nothing. My friend peered too. He pointed far off, where a long shadow stretched dark across the snow. Something was there!

The whip cracked. We shouted to the dogs, and the snow creaked under the sled as the team of huskies plunged ahead.

Quite soon we could see the shape of the airplane with only one wing. A man crawled out of the shadow under the wing and waved. We waved back and shouted again.

It was the plane! When we reached it we unrolled a sleeping bag and put it on the sled for Mr. Benson, since his leg was broken. This meant we must leave the rest of our load of pelts and carvings with the plane, for the dogs could not drag too heavy a sled.

My friend took the sled with the pilot on it back to the camp. Mr. Mackenzie and I waited for more sleds from the camp. He heated water and we had coffee together. We talked of many things.

"This north country!" he said with a smile. "It is the land of the future, and you folk are the People of the Land of Tomorrow.

"Fifty years ago, you would have been a hunter, following the large caribou herds. When the hunting was good, you would have eaten all you could hold, for you knew there would be long, hungry days ahead.

"Now you have been to school and your world is wider. Even those of your people who prefer to live in camps no longer need starve when the hunting is poor. They are learning new skills, and their children will learn more."

"Yes," I said. "Our world is changing."

I wanted also to tell him, "The old men say that long ago the herds of caribou were so vast it took many days for one herd to pass the camp. The children sat in the doorways of the huts or igloos watching the sea of waving antlers. It looked, they say, as if all the people in the world were waving their hands in delight. Now the caribou have moved away.

"My people used to hunt the walrus and the seal, traveling in big light boats. They made these boats of walrus hide. Today they buy boats, and they have motors to take the place of paddles.

"My people are losing many of their old skills. No longer do they scrape and stretch the walrus hide, split it thin, then soak it and stretch the wet slippery skin over a frame of whalebone and driftwood to make a boat.

"Some of the children do not learn the language of our people, with its beautiful songs and tales. There was wisdom in the old ways of our people. It was one of our old women with her inner sight

who helped us find your plane. This was not something learned in school. We must take care not to lose those things of value as we move into the wide world of men."

All that I wanted to say. But it was too much to put into words.

Mr. Mackenzie was looking at me thoughtfully over his coffee cup. He quietly nodded his head.

Then we heard shouts. Up came the sleds from camp. The father of Derek put his arm across my shoulders. Together we walked to the sleds, and soon we were off toward the town.

2. Far North, Far West

Land of "The People"

Far north in the Arctic the continent of North America breaks up, along an uneven shore line, into a fringe of islands. These islands are too numerous to count. Many of them are small and covered with ice, but a few are huge, with mountains rising eight and ten thousand feet above the icy seas.

South of the islands, the northern part of the continent is a wide, empty stretch of cold, treeless plain known as tundra.

For thousands of years the tundra was home only to "The People," as the Eskimos called them-

24

selves. They knew of no other people on earth. They moved about, fishing and hunting seal and whale.

Several thousand Eskimos are still scattered over the northland, most of them living in clusters of huts close to the shores. In recent years, however, groups of pale-skinned men from the south have come to live among them. For the far north is Canada's rich and lively frontier.

Life is changing for Eskimos. Today only about one in ten has ever lived in the kind of domed snow house called an igloo. Most Eskimo children go to boarding school in a settlement. Most settlements have a church or two, some small houses, and a trading post, probably a Hudson's Bay Company store. The red roofs of these Company stores can be seen for miles over the snow. There are about 80 such communities in the Northwest Territories alone.

More and more young Eskimos are getting jobs in settlements and larger towns when they finish school. Boys and young men work in refineries or mines. Girls work in shops, or, with training, as nurses or assistant teachers.

Now and then a young man leaves his job,

Eskimo children, like all of the Canadian young people, now attend school.

turns his back on the settlement or town, and returns to the camp of his family on some lonely shore.

"Men in towns shut themselves away from the world," he says. "A man can live a lifetime in a town and never see the track of an animal leading him on a hunt. Town life is not for me."

Land of Little Sticks

At the southern edge of the tundra, mosses, lichens, low willows, and dwarf birch begin to appear. There are so few warm, sunny days each year in this land that it may take one of these stunted trees a hundred years to grow a foot. The Indians called this "the land of little sticks." Geographers call it the Barren Grounds.

The wide wilderness of these Barren Grounds of northern Canada is rather colorless. Through the long, long winter it is snow-white or gray-brown. The last of the ice does not melt from ponds and lakes until mid-July. By mid-August, the first wind-driven snowflakes warn of another winter's coming.

But during the brief weeks of summer, this bleak land is carpeted with numberless tiny flowers, red and blue, brilliant under a clear sky and reflected in deep blue waters. Over them, clouds of mosquitoes hum. Travelers need all the protection head nets and insecticides can give when they move through the Barren Grounds.

The Polished Shield

Hudson Bay cuts a huge gash deep into the eastern half of Canada. Curving around the Bay in an immense horseshoe is a rocky formation known as the Canadian Shield; it covers almost half the country.

Here, long ago, during the Ice Age, glaciers scraped away most of the soil. Some of the Shield is forested, but there is a vast stretch of bare, scarred, polished rock, pitted with hollows carved

An oil refinery lights the night sky.

by the slow movement of the glaciers. In these hollows countless lakes have formed. Some are brown and boggy with moss; others are connected by clear, shallow streams.

The bare rock of this area is part of the most ancient rock formation found on the surface of the earth. It holds veins and layers of more mineral wealth than men have yet had time to explore. Zinc, lead, copper, gold, radium and uranium are already being mined. Rich deposits of oil, coal and iron have been found.

The Canadian Shield may be a vast storehouse

of mineral wealth, but as landscape it looks bleak. Before World War II, only an occasional canoe skimmed across the moss-brown lakes. A few Indian families wandered there, in search of game. An occasional trapper or explorer made his way through the wilds.

The spread of airplane travel and the mining boom have begun to change that. There are now a few scattered settlements, but the Shield is still mostly a wide wilderness today. There is plenty of exploring still to be done.

Ranges of Peaks

In the western half of Canada, mountains, lakes, and plains are on a grand scale to suit the vast size of this second largest nation on earth.

The immensely long mountain chain of the Andes and Rockies extends north into far-western Canada. At its northerly end, this longest mountain system splits into several ranges, side by side. They tower in ridge after snow-peaked ridge, marching northward in ranks five hundred miles wide.

On the high slopes of the Ice Field Ranges, in this rugged northland, lie the largest glaciers

Geologists help explore the Ice Field Ranges.

outside the polar icecap. Only a few years ago,
those peaks and glaciers were unknown to man.
Today an occasional ski plane skims to a landing
on the ice.

On the lower slopes of the mountains, caribou,
moose, goats, and mountain sheep graze in pas-
tures sheltered by the mountains from wet Pacific
winds.

Those winds spill from 60 to 150 inches of
rain a year on the Alaska side of the mountains.
Because the winds cannot lift water-laden clouds
over the peaks, the Canadian side gets only about
ten inches of rain a year.

It is up in this rugged land, in the Yukon Territory, that much of Canada's gold is mined.

The Green Coast

Farther south, those wet winds keep the island-guarded coastlands of British Columbia moist and green, with thick forests and beautiful flowers. The ranges of mountains that march the length of this area are too steep for much agriculture. In small fertile valleys, however, fruits and vegetables do grow very well against backgrounds of snow-covered peaks. Sheep and cattle range over inland valleys where less rain falls. And forests on slopes of the mountain supply timber for a flourishing lumber industry.

The export of forest products keeps Pacific ports busy. There are good harbors here; they are sheltered from ocean storms by large islands. Between these islands and the mainland lies the coastal waterway known as the Inland Passage.

The busy heart of the west coast industry and shipping is the city of Vancouver. Its fine harbor is sheltered by rugged and richly wooded Vancouver Island. Grain from the prairies, fruit from the mountain valleys, fish from the waterways, lumber from immense forests on the mountain slopes all come into Vancouver by rail or water.

There are many factories for processing the

riches of this green coast, and many steamers hoot as they approach the harbor. Vancouver is Canada's second busiest port as well as a great industrial city. The people of the area are quick to point out that the city, spread over hills above the harbor, is as beautiful as it is busy.

This mountainous far-western region has many beautiful spots, with glacier-green lakes, tall peaks, noble stands of timber, rushing rivers. Many of the loveliest sections have been set aside as national parks for vacationers of today and for the people of tomorrow.

3. The Forest World

Timber!

A keen-eyed young man stops at the foot of a tree and squints upward. This is no ordinary tree, but a giant in a forest of great western trees. Its trunk shoots up in a clean, straight line, vanishing at last among tangled branches. The young man, a rigger with a lumber crew, gives a hitch at his heavy belt and nods his head approvingly. The cruiser has made a good choice.

The cruiser is the man on a lumber crew who marks the trees to be cut by a drive. He has chosen this giant Douglas fir to be used as a spar, to guide the fall of other trees. All around the spar tree in the forest, other trees have been marked by the same cruiser for cutting.

Woodsmen are already busy notching the trees marked for felling, to control the direction of their fall. It is time for this young high rigger to top his spar.

He flings a rope fastened to his belt around the trunk of the giant. When he has fastened the other end, he has a strong rope loop around the tree to help him climb. Up he goes, his cleated boot soles gripping the bark. In less than two minutes, he is up 150 feet. From here he can look up into the crown of branches that soars 200 feet above the forest floor.

The rigger saws off the crown of his giant. As the crown falls away, the tree sways like the mast of a schooner in a storm at sea. This is a dangerous moment for the rigger, but he is used to it.

As soon as the swaying quiets, the rigger attaches guy wires to the trunk. The wires support a long horizontal beam called a boom. Now the spar tree, with its boom, is ready to be used something like a crane in handling nearby logs.

When the trees to be cut have been notched,

Loading a logging truck in a British Columbia forest.

the fellers come up with their power saws. The saws snarl into the wood on the opposite side of each tree from the notch.

"Timber!" shout the fellers, when a giant begins to sway. And everyone stands clear.

Smaller electric saws soon clear away the branches from the fallen tree, leaving a bare round trunk. When this limbing, as it is called, is completed, the log is ready to be moved.

Sometimes wires from the spar are used to lift logs onto a tractor trailer. In other groves, skilled loggers flip logs around with hook-ended poles called peavies. Horses can then drag the logs to water.

Though some logs are trucked out of the forest,

most of them still take a watery road to the mill. They may be floated downstream, chained together into big raft-like booms. Or they may be towed on barges, and then dumped sideways into the water when they arrive at the mill pool.

At the mill pool, the logs are sorted by men using peavies. Some logs will be used for wood pulp, others for newsprint. Still others, straight and thick and of good quality, will be sawed into lumber.

Here go the logs for newsprint. Each one is pushed into a trough that has a toothed chain at the bottom. The chain pulls the logs up a slope to the saws. The biggest logs are cut into planks. Then over rollers and down chutes they go. They splash into the water of a trough called a flume, and there they are ground into a thick, fibrous mush.

The mush is rolled flat and dried. It comes out in big round rolls of newsprint cut just right for newspaper presses. Since most newsprint mills are built beside water, the rolls can be loaded directly onto ships. From Canada, newsprint is shipped all around the world, supplying more than half of the world's needs.

Logs come to this pulp mill by freighter and by rail.

Shadow of Old Trees

The lumber industry is both the biggest and the oldest in Canada. When the first explorers came to this new land, they lived among waters and forests. To build a house, they cut trees for logs. To plant a garden, they cut trees to clear a plot. To earn money, they cut more trees and loaded the lumber onto ships bound for Europe.

The Frenchmen learned early to stack their cut timber on frozen lakes and let the rivers, swollen by spring floods, carry the logs down to the sea. They fastened logs into rafts to float them across

37

quieter waters to small sawmills powered by rushing river water.

When the English began to settle in the New World, they soon learned these lumbermen's ways. In New England they built up a big trade in long straight trunks to be used for masts on sailing ships. They also cut white oak into barrel staves for plantations in the West Indies.

England got most of her lumber from the New England forests until the time of the American Revolution. Then they had to turn to Canada. They did not find white oak in Canada's forests, but they found a wealth of other trees—spruce, pine, fir, cedar, and maple.

By the early nineteenth century, many of the forests of Europe had been pretty well cut over, so there was a larger and larger market for Canadian timber. Small traders who had owned local sawmills became big businessmen. Today this industry produces more goods, uses more electrical power, and pays more wages than any other in Canada.

As people moved west, more and more forests were opened up. Some of the finest are those of British Columbia's mountain slopes with their warm climate and ample moisture from Pacific rains.

The late-nineteenth and early-twentieth centuries brought settlers to the treeless, grassy prairies of Western Canada. Caravans of creaking covered wagons called "Red River carts" rumbled out to new homesteads, and railways that were pushed through served the settlers. The lumber industry supplied timber and planks for new homes, ties for new railways, and fine woods for sturdy furnishings. More and more wood products also went abroad for sale. Down went grove after grove of trees that had taken centuries to grow.

From the air, Canada's forests still look limitless. But lumbermen know that modern crews can move through them fast. The men of the lumber industry are looking to the future. They are taking care to replant seedling trees as they cut. With lookout towers and well-trained crews and warnings to campers, lumbermen are trying to prevent the forest fires that every year waste valuable raw materials of Canada's most important industry.

Conservation is the great new tool of the lumber industry.

A Folk Tale

4. Petit Jacques

It was winter in the woods. Snow lay deep on the ground. It heaped up in white mounds on the branches of the forest evergreens and piled in drifts against the walls of log cabins in the lumber camp.

Out in the woods, the men were hard at work. The sun glinted from the swinging blades of their axes as they hacked deep notches into the trunks of trees. It danced on the sharp teeth of their saws as they slashed the trunks until the forest giants swayed and fell.

The shouts of the men rang out as they chopped,

sawed, and loaded logs. They were all so busy that at first they did not see a stranger approach down the snowy forest trail.

Crunch, crunch—the hoofs of a huge white horse ground into the dry snow. On the back of the white horse sat a small round figure. He looked like a woodsman—plaid jacket, scarlet cap, boots and all. He had a pack on his back, and snowshoes swung at his side. But he was the size of a small, chubby boy.

"Hallo!" called out the small stranger from his seat on the back of the great white horse. "Can you use another hand? I'm here to work."

The woodsmen nearby straightened up and looked around. They looked at the small round figure on the huge white horse, and they laughed until the woods rang.

"Work!" they roared. "What can you do, help Cookie clean up after meals?"

The small stranger slipped down from the horse's back. He stood, hands on hips, feet apart, in the snow, and he looked those rough, tough woodsmen in the eye.

"I'm a woodcutter," said he.

"Oh, you are, are you?" asked one of the

woodsmen, wiping his hand across his mouth to hide his grin. "Well, come on over here. Here's a nice little spruce. Let's see what you can do."

The stranger took an axe from his pack. He spat on his hands and took a swing. How the chips flew! In seconds that trunk was notched, as neat as you please.

He then took a saw from his pack and fitted the blade against the bark of the tree. Sawdust billowed out like smoke. The stranger tapped the trunk and the men heard a warning creak. They scampered like rabbits as the spruce fell down, scattering snow like foam.

The camp boss was on hand by now.

"You're hired!" he cried, clapping the small stranger across his shoulders. And he led him to the office of the camp clerk, to have him sign the roll.

"What's your name?" asked the boss.

"Jacques (zhock)," said the stranger with a merry grin.

The men could not let it go at that. He was *Petit Jacques* (pe-tee-zhock) from then on. That is French for "Little Jack."

Clang! Old Cookie was hammering on his

gong. Petit Jacques filed into the cook house with the rest of the crew for dinner.

They were good eaters, those lumbermen, and the cook was ready for them. He had platters heaped with big chunks of spicy beef, pans of steaming beans, huge bowls of potatoes, pitchers of brown gravy, and great baskets of bread in long crisp loaves.

Soon they noticed that whenever a platter, pan, bowl, or pitcher got to Petit Jacques, it stopped right there. In a moment it was licked shining clean. That small round stranger put away as much food as any ten men!

Then he hitched up his pants and picked his teeth, and back to work he went. He'd notch a trunk, he'd saw it through, he'd whack off the limbs in a fast one-two. Then he'd hoist the log into the air and swing it over his shoulder there. He'd carry those logs all by himself and pile them on a sled like cups on a shelf. He'd harness his white horse to the sled and drive it to the frozen lake before a word was said.

The other men worked in teams; they grunted and heaved to shift those logs so a horse could skid them to a pile. But there was round little Petit Jacques, notching and cutting and heaping up sledful after sledful of logs, all by himself. He'd do the work of a hundred men, then go back to the woods and start in again!

They were strong, proud men in that lumber crew. They fished every spring, they farmed in the summers; and, tough as nails, they spent their winters lumbering. Now, as they waited for a horse to move their logs, their faces darkened angrily at the sight of Petit Jacques. He went stepping by with a great log on his shoulder, whistling as he went.

They would even the score in the bunkhouse,

they vowed! So they started a roughhouse. First came the spider walk. With legs locked around one another's chests, they tumbled and rolled on the floor. But when anyone took on Petit Jacques, the little fellow ended up on top.

Next came a pillow fight. The two fighters sat facing one another on a log sawhorse. They slung pillows at one another's heads. It was a rowdy game. Petit Jacques took his turn against a tough old woodsman.

Biff, biff, biff—the older man slapped his pillow at Petit Jacques. The little fellow bent beneath the blows. But then whack, whack—his pillow slapped back like a whiplash, and down went the tough woodsman on the floor!

Last came the broom pull. One of the biggest, strongest lumberjacks of them all faced Petit Jacques. They sat on the floor, boots sole-to-sole. Then at a signal they both began to pull.

They tugged and they pulled. They sweated and strained. They grunted and wheezed. For a moment the seat of Petit Jacques' pants left the floor. The men all held their breaths. Then Jacques took a deep breath, right down to his toes. He gave a great pull. And headfirst, pell-mell, there came the tough old woodsman sailing through the air! Petit Jacques had won again.

What a cheer the lumberjacks raised for the small round champion of them all! They tossed him in a blanket as high as the rafters. They carried him on their shoulders to the cook house. And for supper Petit Jacques ate as much as any twelve of them.

All winter he worked with that lumber crew. By the time the sun was rolling toward the north and spring was on its way, the lake near the camp was heaped with logs that covered every inch of the ice.

"What a drive we'll have this year!" crowed the men. "No need for dynamite to break the ice! No log jams to send us dancing out on twirling logs with our long, hooked peavies, risking an icy spill. We'll have Petit Jacques to keep things going well."

Petit Jacques just smiled his merry smile and said little, as usual.

Came the first warm day, he sniffed the air. Then he went to the clerk and drew his pay. He stuffed his pack with dollar bills till it bulged like a balloon. Then he swung himself onto his big white horse and slowly rode away.

The men could scarcely believe their eyes.

"Jacques!" they called. "Petit Jacques!"

He turned and waved. They could see his merry smile as he swung his scarlet cap in the air. Then he reached a turn in the forest trail and vanished from their sight.

He has never been forgotten, though, you may be sure. In every northern lumber camp in all of eastern Canada, you will hear of Petit Jacques. And now and then word comes drifting down the wind that he has been seen—of course, riding as always on his great white horse.

5. East from the Rockies

Golden Wheatland

As one moves eastward through the ranges of the Rockies, the land flattens out into prairie country. As far as the eye can see and for a thousand miles beyond, lie level plains. These plains, like the western mountains, extend from Mexico to the Arctic.

For thousands of years wild grasses sprang up fresh each spring as the snows melted on the Great Plains. The grasses grew several feet tall, bending before the breezes. With summer's heat they burst into soft golden heads, only to snap and crumple under the snows of prairie blizzards.

48

Over these grasslands wandered millions of the American bison, more often called buffalo. Family groups of Plains Indians traveled about following the herds. Their tents and food were loaded on frames drawn by horses.

Few of the buffalo or bison remain today, and less than one percent of present-day Canadians are Indians. Some of the tribesmen of the Blood, Blackfoot, Sarcee and Piegan tribes live on the prairie still. Their fathers made peace with the pale-faced settlers. Some Indians live on reserves. Others work on ranches or in towns. But they remember the old days, and in late summer they hold lively festivals. There are tribal dances, singing, and contests. The Indians gather in all the old tribal finery their people wore in the days when they followed the buffalo.

Today, instead of buffalo grass, great fields of wheat run from horizon to horizon on the prairies. Neat clusters of modern farm buildings rise here and there, strung together by electric power lines.

At harvest time huge harvesting machines called combines roar across the fields. Along the railway tracks the towers of grain elevators are filled with wheat ready for shipment.

The wheat fields, which provide Canada's most important crop, extend across much of the southern half of Alberta, Saskatchewan, and Manitoba Provinces. This is not one-crop country, though. Almost half as many acres are planted with oats as with wheat, and many farmers grow barley, sunflowers, and flax. Other acres are grazing lands for cattle and sheep.

These grain farms and ranches are so large that towns and even farm homes are widely scattered. Several cities of more than 100,000 people have grown up on the prairies. Regina and Winnipeg are in the heart of the grain fields. Calgary and Edmonton are young cities that have boomed since the discovery of oil and the opening of the Northland. Between these cities, though, settlements are small and distances are great.

Children on the prairie farms once had rather lonely times. Now farm families are in touch with the outside world; they have telephones, radios, and television as well as all sorts of electric appliances.

The children are picked up by school buses and taken to big new schools that may be miles away. Modern roads span the prairies, so the buses can make good time. Winter blizzards, with strong winds lashing the snow into drifts, occasionally close schools for a day or two, but the children do not mind too much. Summer, they know, will bring long hot days again.

Along the St. Lawrence

East of the prairies, the rocky Canadian Shield curves southward with its deep forests and hidden rivers. This is rough country, with few farms and fewer towns. But to the south and east of it, the country changes again.

Here the St. Lawrence River flows to the Atlantic from the chain of Great Lakes deep in the heart of the continent. Most of the Great Lakes border on both Canada and the United States. The heart of Canada beats along this Great Lakes–St. Lawrence waterway.

It was along the Gulf of St. Lawrence that the first explorers and settlers from Europe landed in what is now Canada. Two-thirds of the people of the country still live along this waterway.

North of the river, the neat farms soon disappear as deep forest closes in. The rounded Laurentian Mountains are covered with timber. Trappers roam there, hunting abundant fur-bearing animals, and lumbermen gather there for winter work. City people crowd the many inns of the Laurentians in winter to enjoy skiing on the long, snowy slopes.

South of the river, the land close to the border of the United States is mostly cleared farm country rather than forests, and it is thickly dotted with towns strung together along good highways. The river itself winds among thousands of small, peaceful islands popular with vacationists.

In the triangle of the lowlands tucked in among the eastern Great Lakes—Huron, Erie, Ontario—lie many of Canada's principal cities, with humming factories and growing sections of apartment homes. Among them is Toronto, the capital of the Province of Ontario and the second largest city in Canada. To the east lies Ottawa, the national capital.

The cities of Canada are so attractive and such pleasant places to live that it is not very surprising that many newcomers to Canada stay in them. Men who have been farmers in other lands often decide to learn to do factory work so they can live in a city or growing town.

French Canada

A thousand miles from the ocean on the St. Lawrence River is Montreal, Canada's largest city. Montreal has grown to be the busiest inland seaport in the world, even though ice clogs it for several months each year.

Down near the harbor, narrow streets and old, steep-roofed buildings still hold some flavor of past times. Here farmers still bring vegetables and cheeses to the open market place as they did 200 years ago. But most of Montreal is modern, a model for city-planners from many lands.

Handsome skyscrapers tower over busy streets. Some buildings house scores of shops along covered promenades, as well as many offices. There are lovely parks, handsome squares, and old avenues whose stately homes are being crowded out by shops and business buildings.

Montreal, whose name is French for the Mount Royal that towers above the city, is the metropolis of all Canada. Downriver 180 miles, however, lies Quebec City, with its old, narrow, twisting, cobbled streets high above the river. It is Quebec City that is the capital of the Province of Quebec and the heart of French-speaking Canada.

Near Quebec City the farms make a pattern of narrow strips along the river; for each settler wanted river frontage for fishing and transportation. Farming villages look like bits of France transplanted, and sound like it, too. Say "Hello" or "Good morning" here and the reply will come back in French, *"Bonjour"* (bohng-zhoor), meaning "good day."

Most lessons in the Province of Quebec schools are conducted in French, though some of their students study English, too. There are a few English-language schools in the province, and

French is also taught to the students there.

Schools are run by two church committees, a Roman Catholic and a Protestant. Since most people of Quebec are Roman Catholics, most schools are Catholic. The village priest, the *curé* (kew-ray), is one of the most important men in the community.

Thirty percent of all Canadians are the French-speaking *Canadiens*. The Province of Quebec is their homeland, though there are communities scattered all across Canada in which French is spoken. Most of the French families have been in Canada for more than 200 years, and are proud of their language and culture. There are French-language newspapers, theaters, and a French television network.

Atlantic Provinces

Canada turns to newcomers from Europe the wide-open welcoming "door" of the Gulf of St. Lawrence. There are some islands that rise from the Atlantic in forbidding, rocky cliffs. Winter storms can swirl and roar wildly about this coast. But the Gulf of St. Lawrence is surrounded largely by rounded hills and gently rolling land.

Hay is an early-summer crop in the Atlantic Provinces.

Deep forests creep down to some stretches of water, whispering and murmuring. When the fogs of spring have cleared away in the face of the warming summer sun, fields of green clover, of nodding hay, and of sturdy potato plants ripen on the slopes above the gulf. Apples redden in many orchards.

In quaint old towns, houses of brick and of wood are shaded by tall trees, and church spires point toward the sky. Between the towns, peaceful farms cover the rolling land. Here life for some still follows old-time patterns.

Fishermen set out from villages located in sheltered coves along the coast. Going to sea in their sturdy boats, they fish for haddock, halibut, herring, and the fingerlings known as sardines.

Back on the shore, barrels stand ready to be filled with fish packed in salt. Lobster pots, which are slatted wooden boxes with loose net tops, are stacked up, ready and waiting for the lobster season.

In the winter, farmers still turn lumbermen. To make a good living on many eastern farms, the farmer needs to do some fishing and lumbering in addition to raising crops.

Lobster pots are vital equipment in fishing towns.

Since World War II, life has changed for many people in the Atlantic Provinces. Factories have grown in number and importance. Minerals have been discovered and mines have been developed to make use of them.

A good many of the swift rivers have been dammed and power plants have been built to provide hydroelectric power to run factories.

Though most of the atomic power plants built thus far are farther west, Canada's Atomic Energy Control Board has started work along the Atlantic coast too.

All these mines and factories and construction projects need workers. Farm boys by thousands have moved into the towns to work at new occupations. Once-quiet towns have grown into busy cities, while along some country roads weeds grow tall in the yards of abandoned farmhouses.

So the Atlantic Provinces, for some years left behind in Canada's surge across the prairies, are now becoming as briskly modern as most of the rest of this vast land.

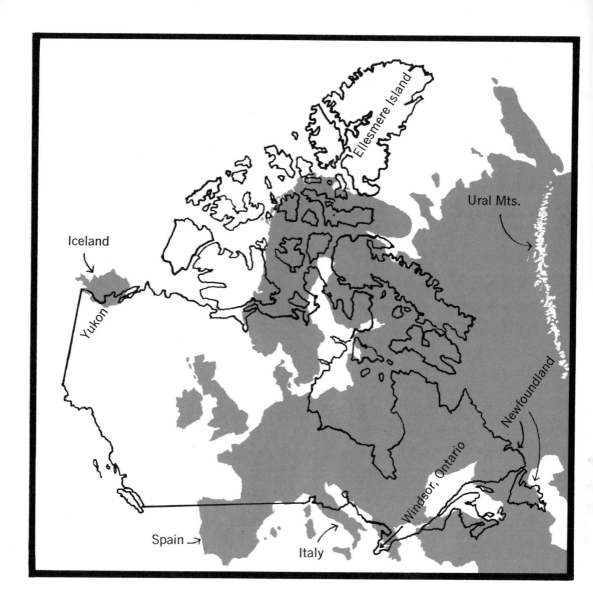

Canada is truly a giant among nations. If the map of Europe is laid over that of Canada, with Iceland over the northwestern corner of the Yukon, the easternmost point of Newfoundland is farther east than the Ural Mountains that separate Europe from Asia in Russia. Canada's Ellesmere Island lies closer to the North Pole than any European territory, but her southernmost point is as far south as Italy or Spain.

6. Sugaring-off

Spring is coming to eastern Canada. This is not a springtime of green grass and woodland flowers. Snow still covers much of the ground; but where the thin sunshine warms open fields, the snow is melting into puddles. That is one sign of spring.

Another sign is smoke curling up from eastern woodlots. Those smoke signals say, to those who can read them, "Sugaring-off time is here!"

Where thick branches screen the sunshine, the woods are still white with snow. On this whiteness, sledge runners have left dark streaks.

If we follow the sledge tracks among the

leafless sugar maple trees, we come upon a busy family scene. Men have already bored holes into tree trunks. They have fixed spouts into the holes and hung buckets from the spouts to catch the rising sap.

The older boys are making the rounds of the tapped trees, collecting filled sap pails. With a pole across his shoulders, a boy can easily carry two of the heavy pails back to the clearing.

In the clearing, a fire is blazing under a huge iron kettle. This is an old-fashioned sugaring-off. Farmers who have big woodlots and make a business of selling maple syrup and maple sugar have modern evaporating machinery to boil down the thin sap. But many families still like the wood-smoke smell and the big picnic lunch in the snow. They like all the lively racing and chasing out-of-doors that are part of the fun of this first celebration of the spring.

The biggest job is keeping the fire going under the big black iron kettle. To boil down the sap from a hundred trees into thick, sweet syrup takes a cord of wood—a stack eight feet long, four feet wide, and four feet high!

The steps of the workers begin to slow as the

sun lowers. The wintry chill creeps into boots and mittens. Then the mother lifts her ladle from the kettle. She pours the first thick drops out onto a clean patch of snow. The drops spread like pancake batter on a griddle, to form flat, round pats of maple sugar. As the young workers taste the melting sweetness of the sugar, they agree that it is reward enough for all the work.

As the family climbs back into the sledge for the homeward ride, one boy says with a sigh, "It would be nice if the syrup just flowed out of the trees, to save us all the work."

"Well," says the father with a chuckle, "that is the way the Indians say it used to happen in long-ago times." And he tells this tale.

The Gift of Nokomis

In the long-ago times, Nokomis or Mother Earth saw how hard the long winters were on her children. She decided to give them a treat. She showed them how to catch the sap of the awakening sugar maple trees in birchbark cups. The sap flowed out as thick maple syrup, rich and sweet. This was Nokomis' gift.

Now Nokomis, Mother Earth, had a grandson, the young god Manabush. He was jealous of his grandmother's affection for humankind. He envied humans the gift of maple syrup. He thought they should have to work for it.

Without a word to Nokomis, Manabush made a plan. He climbed up to the tops of the maple trees. Into each treetop he poured water, to thin the sap.

When men came to collect the gift of sweet syrup in their birchbark cups, all they got was thin, watery sap. To boil the water out, to make the syrup thick and sweet again, men had to learn to make fire. They had to cut trees for firewood and haul the wood. They had to learn to make pots and kettles to hold the sap as it boiled. So the young god Manabush brought work into the world of men. Humankind has had to work ever since.

"That Manabush!" groan the boys. "Oh, for the good old days!"

7. Fishermen All

The Grand Banks

Fishermen in the long, swift ships of the Vikings had chased whales and put down nets for cod off Canada as long ago as the year 1000 A.D.

It was in 1497 that John Cabot and his crew, searching for a western route to the Indies, happened into those waters. They did not find the spices and gold of the Indies, but they did find riches. They found the Grand Banks, the great shallows in the North Atlantic Ocean off the coast of Newfoundland. With the enthusiasm of true fishermen they told of letting baskets down into the sea and bringing them up filled with fish.

By 1530, 500 ships a year were daring the storms of the icy North Atlantic, the blinding fogs and looming icebergs, to sail to the Grand Banks for cod. Even today, in the summers, bright-sailed fishing fleets from Portugal can be seen in Canadian harbors alongside Canadian and and other craft. This is still the richest cod-fishing region in the world.

Fishing is one of Canada's major industries. About 100,000 Canadians make their living by fishing or handling fish. Many more get part-time income from this industry.

Each summer thousands of vacationists drop lines in Canadian waters for sport. But most of Canada's fishing is up-to-date business.

Fleets of sturdy motorized craft work the shallow waters off the Atlantic Coast. Other fleets push out from harbors on the Pacific.

A good many commercial fishermen keep busy catching whitefish and pickerel on the Great Lakes and countless inland lakes. Far northern Great Slave Lake has a big lake trout fishery.

Even in arctic waters, many Eskimos now have

motorboats in which to fish for arctic char, or they have motorized snow buggies to take them across the ice to holes where they have set nets.

There are fish to can, fish to salt, fish to quick-freeze, to pack in ice, and to grind into fish meal or squeeze for oil. Two out of every three fish caught in Canadian waters are sold abroad, to help pay for needed imports.

The Salmon Cycle

Along the Pacific coast, salmon are the main interest of fishermen. Boats from Canada share the waters with others from the United States and Japan during the season. At night their long lines and drift nets skim the surface waters. The salmon swim near the surface at night; during the day they dip down into deeper waters to avoid the light.

Late spring is a good season for salmon fishing, because the warming sun triggers the growth of plankton, tiny sea beings and plants. Small fish feed on the plankton; salmon feed on the smaller fish. The salmon grow rapidly, most of them to a length of two feet and a weight of between five and eight pounds.

One giant type found off Vancouver Island, the Chinook salmon, may weigh from 50 to 100 pounds. Sportsmen by the hundreds come each year to fish for these Chinooks.

The salmon come in to shore and go upriver to spawn, to lay their eggs. Most of them, amazingly, find their way back to the very same river in which they were once spawned. These salmon streams are the mountain rivers that rush down to the Pacific. They race along over rocks and slide down rough, steeply sloping beds. The salmon struggle against the swift current; they fling themselves up the wet rocks. Some are killed, but many reach the shallow spots they seek, to lay their eggs and die.

The eggs develop in their gravel nests, hatching into alevin (al′-e-vin). These tiny fish live, hidden among the rocks and stones at the bottom of the river, feeding on the store of food carried in a yolk sac under their bodies. When the food in the yolk sac is used up, the small fry come out of hiding, looking like very small adult salmon. Then they start the long migration downriver to the sea.

For one to three years they wander in the sea,

67

finding their way mysteriously to the same spot in the ocean from which their parents came. Finally the warming waters of spring lure them back toward the coast. At twilight out from shore come the fishermen in boats; others fish from platforms built above the river mouths. The urge to spawn draws the fish into the mouths of the river, up the streams, and so the cycle completes itself.

Trap in the River

The tide is going out, sucking the tidal waters of the St. Lawrence out into the Gulf. As the level of the water drops, lines of wet fences

poke up into sight. These underwater fences are made of twisted reeds and poles. They are the fish traps of Gaston Le Blanc.

Gaston is a Quebec farmer, with a narrow strip farm that climbs the riverbank to a neat stone house up at the road. He is a good farmer, a thrifty French *Canadien*. But who cannot use a little more honey in the pot? So in season he fishes as well.

His son Pierre is running down to the river now to check the traps. The tide is low; the thick hedge of willow stakes stands up from the mud, black and dripping. Within its walls flop silver fish and dark, snakelike, squirming eels. Those eels had started out to sea on a long migration like that of the Pacific salmon.

Pierre is especially pleased with the catch, because this year he helped build the trap. It must be rebuilt each spring, for the reedy willow wands do not last long. The stout poles can be reused, for they are strong and well anchored in the river bottom. But each spring new willow wands must be cut and woven into thick mesh between the posts, to trap fish and eels.

"Eels?" Gaston smiles at a question about their

use. "*Mais oui* (may we)! But yes! My wife cooks them sometimes, in the old French way. Most we sell, though, to be shipped away. Many go to France, they say, where eels are thought a delicacy."

A twinkle lights his blue eyes. "In the old days, the French *voyageurs* (vwa-ya-zhoors) who traveled these waters and forests liked very much the eels. They cooked with the fat of the eels. The smoked meat they carried for food on their journeys. The skin they split into thin strips and used for twine. The twine they used to fasten the ends of their long hair, one hears." With a big hand he rumples Pierre's shaggy black hair. "If young Pierre here does not get a haircut soon, we'll have to skin an eel for him."

8. Northwest Passage

Age of Exploration

The sturdy, high-prowed boats of the Vikings touched on the rocky shores of North America almost a thousand years ago. These Vikings were the first Europeans to reach Canada, and it seems likely that some of them set up colonies that lasted for several lifetimes. But little trace of them can be found today. Hundreds of years passed before other explorers followed them.

The fifteenth century was the beginning of the Age of Exploration for Europe. Every country, it seemed, was sending out shiploads of explorers searching for routes to India and the Spice

Islands which are known today as Indonesia.

It was such a long sail to these lands from Europe, around the tip of Africa, that men began to try to find a shorter route by sailing to the west. When the long land mass of the Americas was discovered, it seemed at first to be just a barrier on the way to the Isles of Spice. John Cabot, in 1497, was the first of these explorers to reach what is now Canada.

For hundreds of years a search went on for a Northwest Passage around North America to the Western Sea and the Orient. This search was very important in the exploration of Canada.

The Westward Push

Jacques Cartier, one of the earliest French explorers, in 1534 sailed to America and tried going west by traveling up the St. Lawrence River. An Indian chief sent some of his braves out in a canoe, dressed as masked devils, to frighten the strangers away. The men with Cartier were not frightened, but neither did they find the Northwest Passage they sought, though they searched for many years.

Three times in 1576-1578 a brave Britisher

named Martin Frobisher sailed deep into the ice-strewn waters of the Arctic Ocean in search of the Northwest Passage. He touched at huge Baffin Island and other arctic islands. Then, as ice threatened to trap his ship, he turned back, still not having found a sea passage to the west.

Captain Henry Hudson, another British explorer, searched even more stubbornly. He found a narrow passage south of Baffin Island and made his way through it into a vast inland sea now named, in his honor, Hudson Bay.

Hudson was certain there must be a way out to the west. He searched and searched, but only found bleak cliffs and barren shores. Then the weather grew bad and his hardy sailors became

frightened and angry. At last, in 1611, they mutinied and put Hudson, with his son and five sailors, overboard in a small dinghy. The rest sailed back through the straits to warmer waters, leaving Hudson and his friends to lonely death.

Meanwhile the French continued their search. In 1603 the French king sent his royal geographer, Samuel Champlain, to see what he could find. This explorer drew maps and gave names to many landmarks, including a long lake known as Lake Champlain in honor of its discoverer.

Champlain continued his search for a Northwest Passage as far west as Lake Huron. Then he decided that there were riches enough in the forests around him, and he began trading in furs with the Indians.

French vs. English

The push westward continued. French forest rovers and some courageous priests sailed and paddled through the Great Lakes. They continued, by way of wooded lakes and rivers, sometimes carrying their canoes across land, until they reached the source of the Mississippi River.

Other Frenchmen had meanwhile established

a settlement at New Orleans, far to the south at the mouth of the Mississippi. France hoped to claim the whole vast continent, encircling the English colonies along the Atlantic coast. With this empire established, Frenchmen would then push on toward the still-hoped-for Western Sea.

The English also had plans, though. They started somewhat later than the French—both exploring and fur trading. But in 1670 a charter was granted to the Company of Adventurers of England Trading into Hudson's Bay, better known as Hudson's Bay Company. Soon small fortress-like trading posts of the Hudson's Bay Company were dotted along the shores of the bay. Their first shiploads of furs were sent off to England in 1667.

While trappers and explorers pushed westward, back in the East woodlands were being cleared and fields put under the plow by both French and English farmers. Between them there was friction.

Deep in the forests French and English traders, aided by their various Indian allies, attacked and burned one another's trading posts. In the East the French and English settlers fought over farms and town lands.

In 1759, the British seized in battle the French capital of Quebec. The French king's dream of a North American empire died then. But the French people stayed on and multiplied, keeping alive their language and ways of living.

Today France owns only two small islands off the Newfoundland coast, but French and English are both official languages of Canada. There is still lively rivalry and some friction between the two language groups. The ardent young French *Canadiens* now and then stormily demand their independence. But for the most part the two groups live peaceably. In some areas, though, there are villages of Scottish and French families who have lived a few miles apart for 200 years, never speaking to one another because of their different backgrounds.

The Western Sea

The search for the Northwest Passage continued. In 1789 a hardy Scot named Alexander Mackenzie thought he had unlocked the hidden door when he found a great river flowing out of an immense lake now known as Great Slave Lake, deep in the bleak sub-Arctic. The river

down which Mackenzie and his men paddled in eager expectation of reaching the Pacific is now named for Mackenzie. It is the heart of as large a river system as the Mississippi; but Mackenzie called it the River of Disappointment, for it did not lead him to the Pacific after all. It was on the shore of the Arctic Ocean that he stood at last, weary and discouraged.

Mackenzie did not give up, however. He then paddled up another river, called the Peace, toward the western mountains. He and his crew towed their canoe up rapids, clinging to cliffs with bare hands. They cleared trails to carry the canoe through forests. Finally in 1793 they came down the Bella Coola and reached the Pacific Coast.

By this time English sailors had become quite familiar with the Western Sea. Some, like Sir Francis Drake, had reached it by rounding the southern tip of South America, on the trail of treasure-laden Spanish galleons. Others, like George Vancouver, had sailed around the tip of South Africa and across the Indian Ocean into the South Pacific. Vancouver had explored some of the coast of Canada in 1792. So the finding of the Northwest Passage had lost much of its importance. It continued to lure explorers.

In 1847 a British Naval Expedition led by Sir John Franklin was lost, still searching for the Northwest Passage. That disaster started a new round of exploration, by sledge teams as well as ships. One by one the ice-bound islands and straits were explored. But it was not until 1906 that Roald Amundsen on his little *Gjöa* succeeded in making his way from Baffin Bay in the east to the Beaufort Sea in the west. Long before that much easier ways of reaching the Pacific Ocean had been found, and out of the wilderness a great nation had grown.

9. Growth of a Nation

When the British defeated the French in 1759, they were not very clear about just what it was they owned. Much of the vast territory was still unexplored. It seemed likely, though, that British North America would include most of the continent—until some of the colonies to the south revolted in 1776.

Thirteen colonies were lost to the British in this revolution, but still British North America grew and prospered. A good many settlers who were loyal to the British Crown moved north from the newly independent colonies, and became leaders in their new communities. Roads were built, canals were dug, towns grew. Shipbuilding, lumbering, and manufacturing were added to the farming, fishing, and fur trading of early years.

For a number of years there was friction and mistrust between the new United States and British North America. In 1812 war flared up between the United States and Great Britain, and sea battles were fought on the Great Lakes. For some years afterward there was still uneasiness along the Canadian-U.S. border, before today's peaceful cooperation between the two nations was worked out.

Meanwhile, the men of British North America wanted more to say about governing themselves. They sent men to legislatures called provincial assemblies, it was true. But when these men representing the people of the provinces assembled to make laws, they found that they had very little real power.

Irritation grew until in 1837 there were two armed uprisings. Then the British reorganized their North American colonies, calling the largest unit the Province of Canada. This reorganization also marked the beginning of government for the people of Canada by representatives they chose themselves. The Canadian term for this is "responsible government."

This was a good beginning, but it would have been a daring dreamer in 1840 who imagined the great nation of Canada extending all the way across the continent!

A west coast outpost soon came. In 1846 a headquarters of the fur trade was established on Vancouver Island, off the Pacific coast. A few years later gold was discovered on the nearby mainland. That brought action to the little trading post! Roads were hastily blasted through the mountains. Soon stagecoaches were rattling into the wilderness. They carried many prospectors interested only in gold. But they also carried settlers to start the building of another unit of government, a new province.

Settlements were soon appearing across the prairies, too.

Then in 1867 four of the eastern provinces joined together in a union called a Confederation. The powers and responsibilities of government were divided. Some were left with the provincial governments, and others were given to a joint federal government. This Confederation spread across the continent, during the 1870's. A band of provinces stretching from sea to sea was completed when Alberta and Saskatchewan were made provinces in 1905. In 1949 Newfoundland entered the Confederation as its tenth province.

To bring law and order to the great empty territories and to the rough, frontier towns, the government started, in 1873, an organization known as the Northwest Mounted Police.

The Mounties, as this police force soon came to be called, welcomed settlers, rescued travelers from flooded rivers and snowy forests, won the respect of the Indians, put out fires, and escorted the mail. They kept the peace when they could and, when they could not, brought prisoners to trial.

In the years since, their name has been changed to the Royal Canadian Mounted Police; but the Mountie in his stiff broad-brimmed hat and red jacket is still the symbol of law, order, and government in many people's minds. True, today the Mounties on duty rarely wear the famous hats and jackets of their dress uniform. But they have kept their reputation for courage and fairness since the early days.

Canada's Parliament meets here in Ottawa, Ontario.

Like the Mounted Police, the whole Canadian government values its reputation for fairness and concern for the people. At the head of the government is the monarch of Britain, who is also King or Queen of Canada.

The Queen or King appoints an official called the Governor General to act as the Crown's representative. Each province also has a Lieutenant (lef-ten'-ant) Governor appointed by the federal government to represent the Crown.

Canada has a law-making body called the Parliament, made up of two parts or "houses." One is the Senate, whose members are appointed by the Governor General to serve until they reach the age of seventy.

The other house of Parliament is the House of Commons. Its members are elected for a five-year term. If there is a crisis in government, an earlier election can be called.

The working leader of the national government—of all Canada—is the Prime Minister. The leader of the political party with the largest number of elected members in the Canadian House of Commons is chosen Prime Minister. Each province has a Premier, similarly chosen.

Today the governments of Canada and of its provinces work hard to try to assure every one of Canada's people a good life. This includes good wages paid for work done, free education, good medical care, and old-age pensions. The people in turn take a lively, active interest in government and politics.

The Yukon and Northwest Territories still have very few people, widely scattered. So they are governed by groups of persons called commissioners, who are appointed by the federal government. Each territory does elect members to a council, though, and a representative to the House of Commons in Ottawa.

Between meetings of the territorial councils,

84

the local commissioners keep in touch with their people. Judges travel by plane around their huge districts holding court. And the Mounties, who have won the respect and trust of their people, are always at work.

"We respect the people, so they respect us," one mounted policeman explains. He tells the tale of a young Mountie who brought a suspected murderer in by dogsled across hundreds of miles of snowy wasteland. When the two arrived at the station, the young Mountie mentioned that he had lost his rifle before they started on the trek, and he would need another from stock.

"Lost your rifle!" said his superior. "How could you come down through all that wild country at this time of year without a rifle?"

The young Mountie shrugged and smiled.

"Oh, my prisoner had his," he said.

10. School Days

Summer-Time School

Many of Canada's Indians have now settled in or near towns and have learned new ways of living. Their children go to town schools. But some still wander through the woods in small family groups, as they have done for many hundreds of years. For their boys and girls, special schooling must be arranged. These schools, though few, are examples of how Canada cares for all her people.

For nine months of the year, through autumn, winter and spring, Indian families move from camp to camp in the land of lakes and rivers.

Boys help check the trap lines for mink and beaver. They know the woods as a city boy knows the streets of his city. Girls help with cooking and haul water from an ice-covered lake or spring.

The furs of the animals caught in the father's traps are like money to the family. In the late spring the family will head for the settlement. There the furs will be traded for supplies. If the season was good for the trappers, they will buy plenty of salt, sugar, and flour. The children appear in clean dresses or cotton pants and shirts, wearing store-bought canvas shoes. At first they feel a little strange without their familiar buckskins, but the new clothes are part of their summer-time life.

Another part of that life is school. All Canadian children go to school from the age of six until they are fourteen or sixteen, but just where and when they go depends on where they live. These Indians have school only in summer, when they gather in settlements. The government provides a log cabin, a teacher, and books, for it is determined that all its people shall have a chance to learn.

City Schools

Most of Canada's children go to big schools built of brick or stone, with many windows and fenced playgrounds around them. These buildings are in the middle of towns and cities. All around them, along paved streets with neat sidewalks, are the homes of the boys and girls.

In small towns and suburbs, these homes are mostly tidy one-family wooden houses of one or two stories, with sloping roofs. They are set in pleasant lawns green in summer with grass and trees. In big cities, more of the homes are in well-kept apartment buildings where many families live.

Some boys and girls have only a few blocks to walk. If the school is a long way off, a bus picks them up each morning and brings them home again at the end of the school day.

Most of Canada's children grow up and are educated in the closely settled southern part of the country. But in Canada the wilderness is never very far away. It is home to some families; and wherever they are, their children have lessons, too.

Schools on Rails

Arthur and his sister Karen live deep in the forests of northern Ontario. Their father is a railway section man, in charge of fifteen miles of roadbed and track. Where they live, on the section, there are only two other children, not enough for a school.

Every four weeks a train comes tooting into camp with a special car. The car is switched off onto a siding, and a young man soon appears in an open doorway at one end of the car.

At the sound of the whistle, Arthur and

Karen snatch up their books and the lessons they have been doing at the kitchen table. For this is the school car.

The school car and the schoolmaster stay in the settlement for a week. Karen and Arthur and the other children have lessons every day. Two children from the next section of track hike miles to the school every day.

The car is fitted with school desks, blackboards, maps, and a library from which the boys and girls can borrow books. On one wall the schoolmaster displays pictures his students have painted. He chooses one of Karen's to add to the display. On another wall is a map of Canada. It shows the railway line, and there is a colored pin for each child on the school car route.

The schoolmaster tells Karen and Arthur about the other children he teaches. He tells them about children in the Far West who go to school in classrooms built in buses instead of rail cars. He tells them, too, about huge city schools he has seen with hundreds of children.

"Too many!" think Arthur and Karen. "We would not like that!"

Church and School

Everyone in Canada may go to whatever church he chooses, or to none at all. Most people, French, English, Scottish, Russian, German, or Dutch, are Christians. They may belong to the Church of England, the Free Church of Scotland, the Roman Catholic Church, the German Lutheran, Russian Orthodox, or some other branch of the Christian Church.

Some Bible lessons are taught in all the schools of Canada, and in some provinces the schools are operated by the churches. All schools in the Province of Quebec are church schools.

Each province governs its schools in its own way. Wherever there are communities of French Catholics, they may have schools that teach in their own language and that teach their own religion. The only requirement is that every child should go to school. Today tens of thousands of young Canadians go on to colleges, universities, or technical schools.

By bus, train, airplane, or dogsled, Canada manages to bring children and schools together. Today 97 percent of all Canadians, young and old, can read and write.

11. From Sea to Sea

Turkey Tracks

It was the age of railroads that made Canada a nation. Railroads had spanned the United States since 1869. The Canadians were determined that they too could build one to unite their far-flung territories.

The government was so eager to help that it offered to grant a right-of-way 20 miles wide all across the country to speculators if they could build the railway through it.

The right-of-way led through some of the continent's most rugged mountains. So much rock had to be blasted to push through the road of rails that the builders set up a dynamite factory of their own to make the explosives near at hand.

They used river canyons where they could, chopping narrow shelves for the railway into canyon walls. Where mountains were too tall for the road to go over them, the men blasted tunnels through. Deep ravines were crossed with bridges supported by timbers.

Men slaved and sweated; some sickened and died, but the railway pushed on. By the end of the 1880's the long line of "turkey tracks," as settlers called the slender trail of ties and rails, reached the prairie. For a thousand prairie miles the going was easy, across level ground.

Patchwork of Peoples

Once the railway was in, the company began to sell off the adjoining land that the government had given it. The government also offered some land free to settlers. People, hearing that they could now ship their crops out by rail, began to appear in trains of covered wagons or by stage coach, to start homes on the cheap new grasslands.

Newcomers lived in their wagons or in tents

while they planted their first crops of oats, potatoes, and turnips, and cut wood for their first winter. Once the crops were in, they built houses of turf.

In later years, families moved from those small turf shelters into neat wooden homes. They soon added, for each cluster of houses, a saw mill and a flour mill.

As towns grew and farms multiplied, with herds of fat cattle grazing on grasslands, the settlers added cheese factories, schools and small libraries to their villages. Since more than half of the people of the prairies were new Canadians who had come from different European lands, many of these towns have a European flavor.

After the great rush of settlers in the early 1900's, there was a quiet time. Then, after World War II, people seeking new homes and a new chance in life headed for Canada again. More than two million newcomers arrived from more than forty countries, during the next twenty years.

The largest group were still from the British Isles—England, Scotland, and Ireland—but Germans, Ukrainians, Scandinavians, the Dutch, and Poles together now make up fifteen percent of Canada's total population. All have brought and maintained some of their own customs and ways.

"Canada is not a melting pot," Canadians say, comparing their country to their neighbor to the south. "It is rather a patchwork of different peoples, fitted together to form a pleasant pattern with many colorful bits still clear."

It is the railways that stitch together this patchwork of peoples.

Wheels Across the Land

Railways are still expanding in Canada. Two lines now cross the continent from coast to coast, passing through most beautiful scenery in the Canadian Rockies. Lines run northward too. One runs from British Columbia into the gold country of the Yukon, another from the grain fields of the prairies north to the grain port of Churchill on Hudson Bay, and a third through the wilds of Newfoundland and Quebec to the great iron range of Ungava Peninsula.

Now men speak of building giant pipe lines containing endless belts. On these, chunks of ore from the mines or other heavy goods could be carried across the miles, safe from weather.

Canada's southland is criss-crossed with hard-surfaced highways and quieter country roads. More than a million heavy trucks carry food to market or raw materials to factories. Most families have automobiles, too, that they use on the highways and byways, not only for workaday errands but for vacation trips.

The Trans-Canada Highway runs from coast to coast, nearly 5,000 miles. And a new Alaska Highway, built cooperatively with the United States, crosses western Canada to connect Alaska with the main body of the United States.

Almost half of Canada is difficult territory

New industries like this chemical plant in New Brunswick demand modern transportation for marketing their products.

for road building or road travel, though. So waterways are very important too.

Water and Ice

Canada has busy ports on both the Atlantic and Pacific Oceans. Many of the exports that keep her people busy and prosperous go out through these ocean ports. Coastal steamers chug along both coasts, too, serving fishing towns on off-shore islands and beside mainland coves.

More unusual are the Canadian inland waterways. On the western shore of Hudson Bay is Churchill, Canada's most northerly port. Its tall grain elevators rise over bleak tundra. Prairie

97

wheat is loaded from these elevators onto big freighters for the icy North Atlantic crossing after a steam up through frigid Hudson Bay.

Still more important is the Great Lakes–St. Lawrence Seaway. All but the largest ocean liners can now steam deep into the heart of the continent. This is possible thanks to a great joint construction project of the United States and Canada. Montreal, Canada's busiest port, lies a thousand miles from the ocean along the St. Lawrence. But there are also busy lakeports shipping loads of iron ore, wheat, and coal at the rugged western end of Lake Superior, 2,300 miles from the Atlantic Ocean.

Most arctic settlements depend a great deal upon waterways, too. It is a lively day when a supply ship comes into port, or when the toot of a whistle tells that a sturdy tug is ready to depart, towing a train of loaded barges.

"The trouble with waterways," Northerners will tell you, "is that the season of open water is so short. It's true that we don't have as much snow in the Arctic as you might expect, but we have ice! Winds that can freeze a careless man in a couple of minutes start sweeping down from the North Pole in August. They freeze the rivers fast, and the ice pack soon blocks the Arctic Sea."

Before you can sympathize, the Northerner's eyes begin to glow. "You've heard of the nuclear submarines?" he asks. "One crossed the Arctic Sea under the ice without surfacing once. That's the answer to our water transport! We must have underwater tugs, to tow underwater barges under the ice to the open ocean."

Trails Across the Sky

For the present, it is easier to travel by air than underwater. The airplane has made the settlement of the Arctic possible.

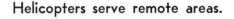

Helicopters serve remote areas.

Workers in new mining towns, refineries, and other northland settlements are old hands at air travel. They and their families fly to their jobs and fly out on holidays. They fly on fishing weekends and hunting trips. They fly on business errands.

Eskimos who may never have seen an automobile or a railway train are flown to a hospital if they are ill. Their children may be flown to school.

Supplies are flown in to remote settlements so that families can have fresh foods, new dance records, and magazines.

Judges fly 25,000 miles a year to hold court in Eskimo huts, on fishing boats, or in parked airplanes. Prospectors looking for minerals go by helicopter. Doctors fly to call on their patients. Priests fly around their vast parishes, conducting services. The Royal Canadian Mounted Policemen often fly to trouble spots, perhaps with first aid kits in their hands. The airplane is the most useful means of travel for the men of the Arctic. It has brought the northland into touch with the modern world, within reach of the cities of the south.

A Story

12. The Gypsy Show

"I am sorry, Paul," Mrs. Dionne said to her son with a little worried sigh. "I know summer is a hard time to move to a strange city. When school starts, you will make friends soon enough."

"Oh, it's all right." Paul tried to sound cheerful, but his steps dragged as he left the apartment and started toward the park.

His mother and father had tried hard since they had moved to Montreal to help him like the place. They had taken him to Beaver Lake and the big park there, and up to the top of Mount Royal in a little red, white, and blue train. Kid stuff, but Paul had to admit it had been fun. The view over the city and up and down the river, off into the hazy distance, was great, if you liked views.

They had gone to lunch in a big restaurant at the top of a towering building on shining new Place Ville-Marie (Plass Vee-ya Ma-ree), a big square surrounded by skyscrapers.

They had strolled along narrow old streets down near the harbor, which was lined with ships from many lands. They had been to the zoo, to Ile Sainte Helene (Eel Sangt Ai-lain) out in the river. They had strolled through the storybook Enchanted Village in La Fontaine Park and through museums. Oh, it was a great city, Paul admitted gloomily. But it was a lonesome place in the summer if you did not have friends.

Paul had seen the school where he would go in the fall, beside the twin-spired neighborhood church. The school just looked big and bleak and empty during vacation.

His father said, "Won't it be great, Paul, to be able to ski this winter, just a ten-minute walk from home, right on the slope of Mount Royal? And think of the ice hockey games."

Paul supposed winter would be great. But that

did not help the lump of loneliness inside him right now, on a bright summer afternoon.

"Go over to the playground," his father had said at breakfast this morning. "Meet some of the boys. You have to do a little something for yourself, you know, son."

Sure, but that was not so easy, when all the other boys knew one another and you were the only stranger.

Paul scuffed at a fallen leaf on the park path and tried not to listen to the happy voices all around him. It was then he heard the music.

Over in the playground, a long trailer truck was parked. That was where the music came from. Trailer trucks did not thrill Paul; they usually were just on their way to or from some factory. This one looked different, though; it was painted in broad stripes of red and white. Boys and girls were clustering around it, shouting excitedly.

Paul circled at a distance. He did not want to look eager. As he circled, he noted a strange thing.

On the trailer's far side, the mid-section of its wall had folded out flat on the ground. In place of that section of wall, full red curtains hung.

"Why, it's a stage!" Paul whispered to himself. "Gosh, if we'd only had something like this back home for the plays we used to give!"

The tinkling of a merry melody seemed to pull his feet across the grass toward the trailer. A girl who looked like Paul's big sister Anne was playing a piano beside the stage. Two young men were talking with the boys and girls who crowded around. Somehow, Paul found himself in the circle.

"You look like a good worker," one of the dark-haired young men said, with a smile. Paul realized with a start that the smile was for him. "Will you have a look around?" The young man was waving Paul with a small group through the curtains at the back of the stage.

For a moment it seemed very dark back there, after the sunlight of the park. As Paul blinked, the small backstage grew brighter.

In front of him dangled Venetian blinds with pictures of houses and trees painted on them. "Our stage sets," the young man explained with a wave of his arm. "Just pull the cord, and you move from Russia to Paris."

104

He gave a tug, and with a clicking sound the blinds flipped over to another scene.

"Look down here, this is the control center," said the guide, opening the door to a small crowded room. Paul caught a glimpse of a phonograph and a board full of light switches.

"Over on the other side are the dressing rooms. You like to play parts in costume, eh?"

There was a small crowded table with a mirror above it, brightly lighted. There were folding chairs heaped with capes and plumed hats. A wonderful smell of fragrant greasepaint and powder and old cloth tickled Paul's nose.

"How would you like to wear this in tonight's play?" the young man was asking. He was holding out a dark green cape and a big three-cornered hat.

"Me?" whispered Paul. "Great! What do I do?"

"Work," grinned the young man with a shrug of his shoulders. "We have need for six helpers for tonight's play. First we have a short time to show you all how this theater works."

"What is it called, your theater?" Paul asked.

"*La Roulotte* (roo-lot)," said the young man. "The gypsy caravan, so to say."

"A gypsy show!" Paul echoed, and he drew the first deep breath of pure happiness he had breathed in Montreal.

That was the beginning of a magic day for Paul. At last that evening he stepped out onto the bright stage, in his flowing cape and big hat. Out in the darkening park, he heard the rustle of the audience. He knew his mother and father were there, though he could not see them. But he did not have time to think much about them.

He just knew that this was what he wanted to do all his life—act!

Next morning, Paul could scarcely finish his breakfast, he was in such a hurry to get back to the park. He raced up the path, then stopped short. He could not believe his eyes.

The trailer was gone! Not so much as a chip of red and white paint lay on the crumpled grass where it had stood.

All around, boys and girls were busy at games and craft projects. But the brightness had gone out of the day for Paul.

"Hello, there," said a voice behind him.

Paul turned to face a tall young man with a tanned face. "Michael is my name," the young man said. "Glad to see you back. You were great last night."

"Where has it gone?" Paul asked.

"La Roulotte? I don't know just where it is today. The troupe plays a different park or playground every day through the summer, you know. They pick up new helpers every day."

"But when will they be back here?"

The young man rubbed a hand over his short hair. "Don't know exactly," he admitted. "Late in the summer, I'd guess. I have the schedule somewhere."

"Oh," said Paul, feeling hollow. He turned away.

"Stay around," Michael invited. "I'm in charge of the summer program on this playground. We do some shows of our own, have some good workers. But I could certainly use a good helper. How about it?"

"Well. . . ." Paul thought longingly of the red and white trailer.

"If you like the work here this summer," Michael explained, "maybe when winter comes you will want to work after school with us in *le Theatre de Quatre Sous* (tay-a-tr da kaht' soos), the Theater of Four Sous. That is the French name, since most of us in the Roulotte troupe are French. The English name is the Tupenny Theatre. Four sous is even less than two pennies, though!

"We work hard there, but we learn about lighting, makeup, painting scenery, and all of the things that go to make up the magic of the theater."

"Great!" said Paul.

"The Quatre Sous supplies members of the troupe for La Roulotte summers, and a good many people go on to work on television, radio, and on the stage.

"Right now, though, we'd better get to work right here!" Michael finished with a laugh.

Paul went to work. He kept on working, summers and after school. If you watch Canadian television, you may see him there, still happily at work.

He has not had time to be lonely since that long-ago day when first he saw the red and white gypsy trailer in the park.

Index

110

Meet the Author

Jane Werner Watson has based her study of Canada on a wide range of personal contacts and experiences. She has cruised on the Gulf of St. Lawrence on a freighter, stopping at small isolated ports, has driven through the rich St. Lawrence lowlands, and has traveled across the prairies, marveling at the beauty of the Rockies from bus, train, and hiking trail.

To the task of turning these experiences into a book, Mrs. Watson brings competence acquired through the writing, editing, and compiling of more than 200 books for young readers from picture-book age to the scientifically-minded teens. Her range of subject matter has been encyclopedic — from atomic power to Bible stories, from merry-go-rounds to dinosaurs. Within this Garrard series, *Canada* now joins *India, Iran, Ethiopia, Thailand, Nigeria, Peru, Egypt,* and *Greece* — all based on Mrs. Watson's wide-ranging travel experiences backed by thoughtful study.

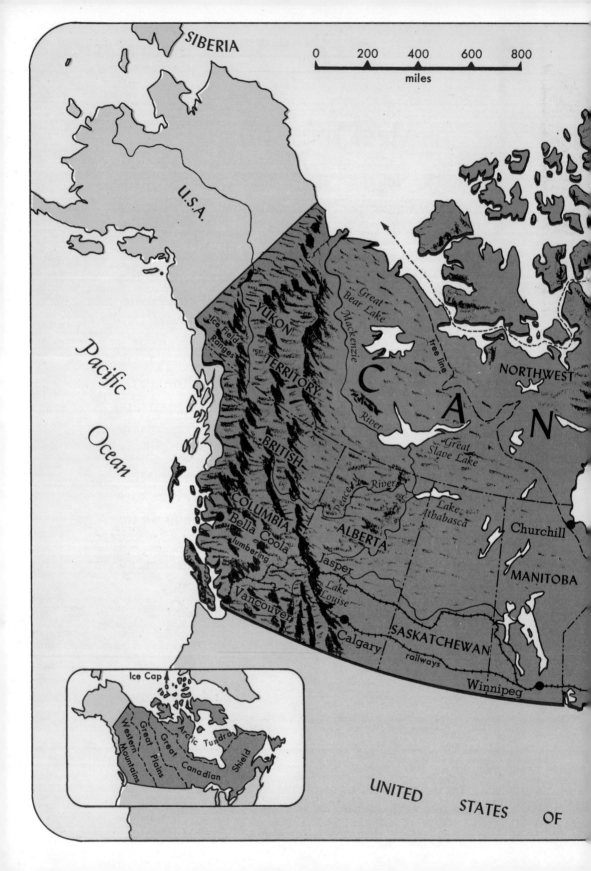

SIBERIA

0   200   400   600   800
miles

U.S.A.

Pacific

Ocean

YUKON

TERRITORY

Ice Field
Ranges

Great
Bear
Lake

Mackenzie

tree line

NORTHWEST

C A N

River

Great
Slave Lake

BRITISH

Peace   River

River

Lake
Athabasca

Churchill

COLUMBIA

ALBERTA

Bella Coola

lumbering

Jasper

MANITOBA

Vancouver

Lake
Louise

Calgary

SASKATCHEWAN

railways

Winnipeg

Ice Cap

Western Mountains

Great Plains

Great Canadian

Arctic Tundra

Shield

UNITED   STATES   OF